Spectacular Sports

Motocross

Rational Numbers

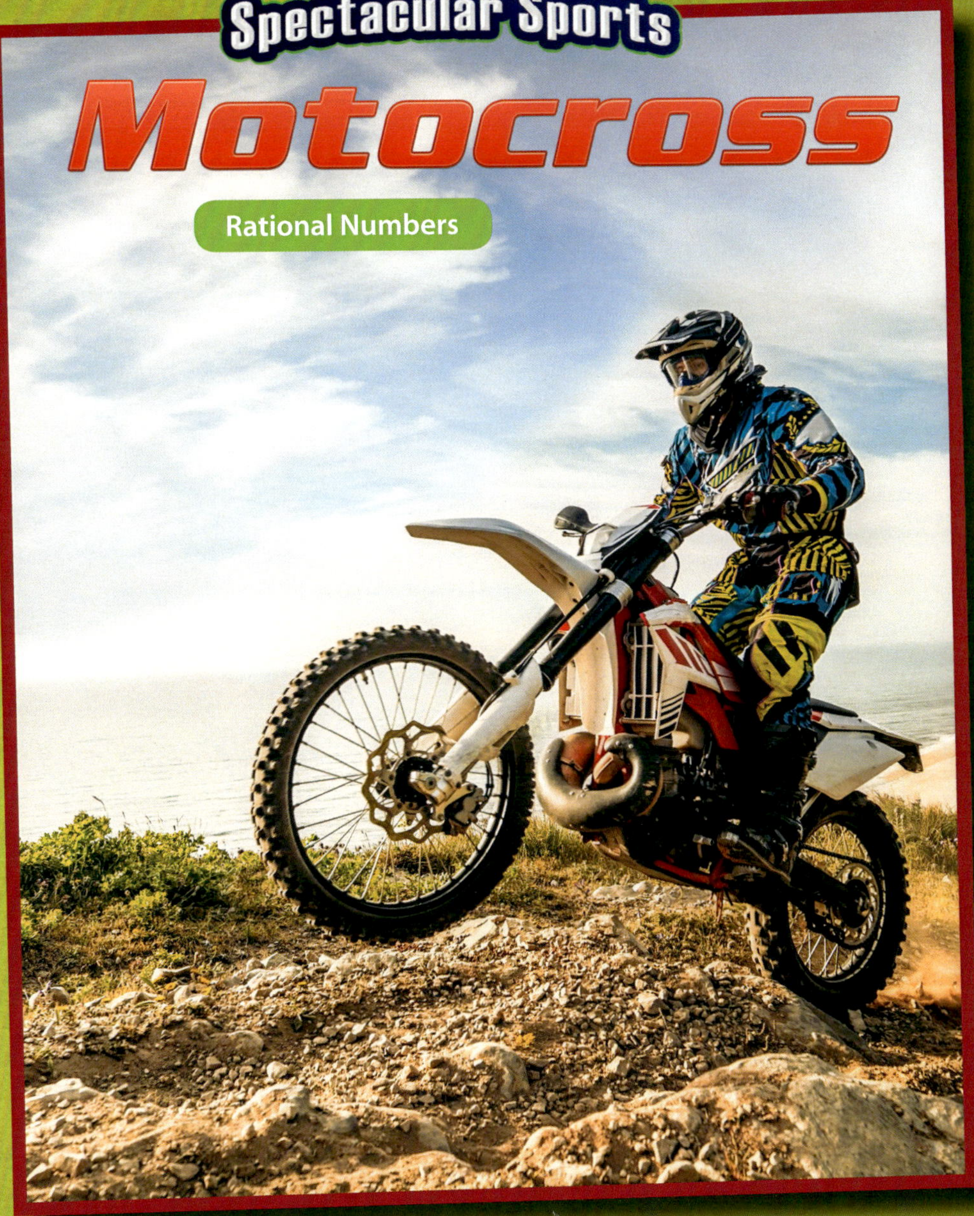

Michelle Lee, M.A.

Contributing Author

Alison S. Marzocchi, Ph.D.

Consultant

Colleen Pollitt, M.A.Ed.
Math Support Teacher
Howard County Public Schools

Publishing Credits

Rachelle Cracchiolo, M.S.Ed., *Publisher*
Conni Medina, M.A.Ed., *Editor in Chief*
Dona Herweck Rice, *Series Developer*
Emily R. Smith, M.A.Ed., *Series Developer*
Diana Kenney, M.A.Ed., NBCT, *Content Director*
Stacy Monsman, M.A., *Editor*
Michelle Jovin, M.A., *Associate Editor*
Fabiola Sepulveda, *Graphic Designer*

Image Credits: pp.4–6, p.8, p.10 (left), p.11, pp.13–17, pp.25–27 Courtesy Susan Jovin; p.7 Jeff Gross / Getty Staff; p.9 Courtesy Bert Jovin Sr.; p.23 B.Stefanov / Shutterstock. All other images by Shutterstock and/or iStock.

Library of Congress Cataloging-in-Publication Data

Names: Lee, Michelle, author.
Title: Spectacular sports. Motocross : rational numbers / Michelle Lee.
Other titles: Motocross
Description: Huntington Beach, CA : Teacher Created Materials, 2019. | Includes index. | Audience: Grade 4 to 6. |
Identifiers: LCCN 2018047787 (print) | LCCN 2018055481 (ebook) | ISBN 9781425855260 (eBook) | ISBN 9781425858827 (pbk.)
Subjects: LCSH: Motocross--Juvenile literature. | Numbers, Rational--Juvenile literature.
Classification: LCC GV1060.12 (ebook) | LCC GV1060.12 .L44 2019 (print) | DDC 796.6/22--dc23
LC record available at https://lccn.loc.gov/2018047787

We at Teacher Created Materials would like to thank Bert Jovin for his time and expertise in making this reader possible. We would also like to thank his family, Bert Sr., Susan, Kristina, and Carmen, for their contributions and support.

Teacher Created Materials
5301 Oceanus Drive
Huntington Beach, CA 92649-1030
www.tcmpub.com

ISBN 978-1-4258-5882-7

Table of Contents

Getting Ready to Race

Meet Bert Jovin, an **amateur** motocross rider. Motocross is a high-intensity **dirt bike** race that takes place outdoors. Riders not only have to race through the course, but they also have to avoid and overcome obstacles, such as thick trees, tough **terrain**, tight turns, and oftentimes, mud…lots of mud.

Jovin takes his time preparing for each race. He needs to know what he will be facing each weekend, so he can modify his training **regimen**. If Jovin knows the racetrack will have a lot of trees, he may practice riding in forests. Other races are on beaches, so Jovin will change his tires to better grip the sand.

Whatever the terrain may be, Jovin has to be prepared. He gets ready as early as he can for a race. Sometimes, he has months to prepare, while other times, a last-minute weather change can force him to adjust his training. Usually though, Jovin has about a week in between races. That gives him about five days to do all of his necessary preparations. Let's follow Jovin during a typical week as he prepares for a race.

Jovin puts his gear on.

LET'S EXPLORE MATH

One morning, Jovin trains for three and one-quarter hours for an upcoming beach race.

1. Write his training time as a decimal. Then, write it as two different fractions.
2. Plot Jovin's training time on a number line like this one. What strategies can you use to make sure you are accurate?

$$\longleftarrow -5 \quad -4 \quad -3 \quad -2 \quad -1 \quad 0 \quad 1 \quad 2 \quad 3 \quad 4 \quad 5 \longrightarrow$$

Motocross races are outdoor contests where riders race on dirt bikes. Each race lasts just over 30 minutes, and there are two races for each **class**. Another dirt bike sport, called supercross, is similar to motocross, but it takes place in a stadium. And a third related sport is arenacross, which, as the name suggests, takes place in an arena. Motocross, however, is something unique. It combines the **technicality** of an indoor race with the elements of nature.

Motocross racers ride in whatever conditions they are given. They race in blazing heat and in pouring rain. They race in dusty deserts and through muddy swamps. Oftentimes, it is the state of the track, and not the track itself, that is the biggest challenge for riders.

That is what happened at the 2006 professional motocross race in Millville, Minnesota. A huge storm hit between the first and second races, turning the track into a swamp. Rider Ricky Carmichael jumped into first place. As mud started ruining dirt bikes all along the track, Carmichael's bike kept going. By the end of the race, he had passed every other racer a second time. No one had ever done that before. And most likely, no one will ever do that again.

Jovin crosses the finish line in an arenacross race.

Ricky Carmichael celebrates after winning a race in the 2007 X Games®.

LET'S EXPLORE MATH

Imagine that a motocross racer is making great time early in a race. She averages $2\frac{1}{2}$ minutes per lap. Then, a light rain begins. Her average time increases to 3 minutes per lap late in the race.

1. Plot the racer's early and late race averages on a number line like this one.

   ← –5 –4 –3 –2 –1 0 1 2 3 4 5 →

2. Which time is farther from 0 on the number line?
3. How can you tell which time is an integer?

Prepping His Bike

Luckily, Jovin has never had to race on a track like the one at Millville; however, he does encounter mud on most racetracks. Preparation for these races is key. Before race day, Jovin studies the weather, his opponents, the track layout, and whatever else he thinks might help him. He changes the setup of his bike depending on which track he will be racing.

Jovin's tires are perhaps the most important **facet** of his dirt bike. Jovin lives in Oregon, where it rains for about half of the year. That means many of the racetracks on which he competes will have mud. For muddy races, Jovin puts tires with a wide **tread** on his bike, so mud doesn't get packed in them. If this happens, the tires will not have good **traction**, which can be very dangerous.

Jovin also protects the engine of his dirt bike. If mud gets around his engine, it could get too hot, and the dirt bike could **seize** up and stop running. Jovin fixes that problem with foam. Foam is light and does not add weight to his bike, but it is absorbent enough to soak up mud before it hits the engine.

Jovin's dirt bike may get muddy, but his preparation will keep it running.

Foam around the air filter stops dirt from mixing with the fuel.

LET'S EXPLORE MATH

Racers have an interesting use for cooking spray. They spray it all over their bikes, but especially under the fenders. This prevents mud from sticking. Built-up mud makes bikes heavier and more dangerous over jumps. The spray not only keeps bikes cleaner, but it keeps them safer too.

Imagine that racers spray their bikes with cooking spray to get ready for a race. Kristina uses 28.349 grams, Rosa uses 28.094 grams, and Scott uses 28.4 grams. Which racers use the greatest and least amounts of cooking spray? Use words, numbers, or pictures to explain your thinking.

For muddy races, Jovin also needs to make sure he stays safe, which he does by changing his gear. He might wear a shirt under his jersey to keep his skin from getting showered with mud. He might wear thicker gloves so that any flying rocks that hit his hands will not hurt as badly.

Jovin also takes care of his vision by putting more tear-off strips on his goggles for mud races. Tear-off strips are plastic strips on Jovin's goggles. If mud gets on the top tear-off strip, Jovin can rip it off and have a clear line of vision. Jovin always rides with tear-off strips, but for muddy races, he puts on a lot more. If he runs out of tear-off strips, he might have to pull out of the race to avoid getting hurt.

In the days before a race, Jovin makes sure he has everything he needs. From packing foam in his dirt bike to adding tear-off strips to his goggles, he does everything he can to stay safe on the racetrack.

motocross gloves

Jovin's muddy helmet and goggles after a race

Jovin gets muddy during a race, but his tear-off strips keep his vision clear.

Prepping His Body

Jovin's dirt bike is not the only thing he needs to take special care of before a race—his body is just as important. Jovin makes sure he is ready to race by eating right, exercising, and staying **lithe**.

Eating Right

To perform at his absolute best, Jovin needs to make sure he eats right. Most adults burn about two thousand calories a day. But on race day, Jovin will burn around five thousand calories! That means he has to eat well leading up to the race so he is ready to perform when it counts.

Jovin grows his own fruits and vegetables in his backyard so that the food he eats is as fresh as possible. He also eats lean proteins, such as chicken and fish, to help strengthen the muscles he uses while training. His arms, legs, and torso get an intense workout every time he rides. Jovin's diet helps him take care of sore muscles and keeps him feeling healthy and ready to ride.

Jovin balances his plate like this.

Jovin enjoys a healthy meal after training.

Before a race, Jovin also makes sure he drinks plenty of water. Each motocross race usually lasts about 30 to 45 minutes, and each rider will compete in at least two races a day. During races, Jovin perspires a lot, so if he does not drink enough water, he will become **dehydrated**. Most people drink about eight cups of water a day. Jovin drinks about three times that much on race day. He also has to make sure to drink enough leading up to a race. That way, his body has water stored that it can use when Jovin starts to sweat.

Jovin and his friends take a break during a forest ride.

Exercising

Most of Jovin's exercise comes from riding his dirt bike. He likes to go on long rides that can last up to five hours as he winds through forests and crosses streams. However, Jovin also stays active in other ways. Some days, he may climb a rock wall that he has set up, or he may go swimming against a **current** in a river to build up his muscles and his **endurance.**

LET'S EXPLORE MATH

The water Jovin gains by drinking can be represented with positive numbers. The water Jovin loses by sweating can be represented with negative numbers. Use a vertical number line like this one to track Jovin's water gains and losses.

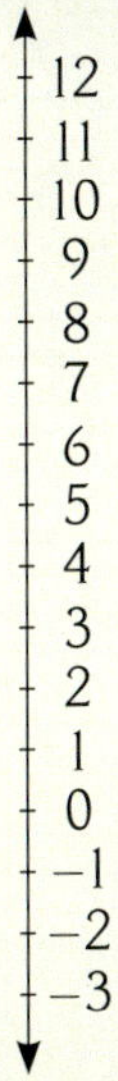

Jovin starts his day by drinking 8 cups of water. He is a bit nervous on his way to the course and sweats 1 cup. Before the race starts, he drinks 2 more cups. During the first race, he sweats 7 cups. He drinks 3 more cups between races. During the second race, he sweats 6 cups.

1. What is the starting point? What does this mean?
2. How can you tell whether Jovin lost or gained water at the end of the day?

Staying Lithe

Jovin also does yoga to prepare for race day. He is not alone in that. Many athletes practice yoga because it teaches them to stretch their bodies, to be flexible, and to control their breathing. Those are very important things for motocross racers to remember to do during a race. When Jovin lands a jump, the impact **jolts** his body. By staying flexible, his body can absorb these impacts better. That makes Jovin much less sore after a race. Also, during races, riders often bump each other. Keeping flexible helps Jovin stay on his bike when he is bumped. Motocross races are high-intensity events. It's important for Jovin to breathe normally even during the most thrilling and dangerous moments.

Yoga also helps Jovin improve his strength and **coordination**. Those two qualities are important when he's riding. If Jovin loses his balance on a jump, he can hurt himself. In the past, he has had deep cuts and broken bones from crashes. Jovin wants to avoid any injuries. Stretching his muscles and doing yoga help him feel confident that he can stay upright while riding.

Jovin stretches his oblique muscles.

Jovin stretches his tricep and deltoid muscles.

Race Day

After all Jovin's preparations are done, it is finally time to race. Races are on the weekends, with the professional racers competing on Saturdays and amateurs on Sundays. By the time Jovin gets to the track on Sunday morning, it has played host to over 20 races. The track is definitely not in **pristine** condition. Jovin will have to deal with mud patches and **ruts** that have built up during Saturday's races.

Moto 1

The first race, or Moto 1 as it's called, takes place early in the day. Jovin lines up at the starting gate and looks out over the long stretch of straight track before it veers sharply to the left. Jovin knows that in a mud race like he's facing, getting a good start is **imperative.** If he does not, he will be stuck at the back of the pack. If that happens, Jovin will get hit with mud and rocks for the next 30 minutes. However, if he gets a good start, he can hopefully build up a gap between him and the rest of the racers and avoid the spray of mud and rocks.

Motocross racers line up at the starting gate.

A track worker stands in front of the starting gate and holds up a sign that reads "30." Then, he rotates the sign sideways, which tells the riders that within the next 5 seconds, the race will begin. Jovin leans forward in **anticipation**; this is what all of his preparation has been for. After what feels like forever, the gate drops and the race begins.

As Jovin and the other riders race forward, they hit handlebars and bump one another. Jovin passes most of the other riders and enters the first corner near the front of the pack. Jovin knows that the first corner of any racetrack is one of the most dangerous. As a group of around 20 riders all try to fit into a narrow turn, there are bound to be crashes. That is why getting a good start is necessary in motocross. Jovin has been practicing his starts. All that hard work pays off, and Jovin misses the opening corner crash. He turns left as riders pile up behind him. Jovin gives his bike the **throttle**, and just like that, he is in third place.

Motocross racers wait for the track worker to hold up the 30-second board.

LET'S EXPLORE MATH

Suppose that as Jovin approaches a corner, he is neck-and-neck with some of his opponents. Draw a number line like this one. Use it to track their positions and answer the questions.

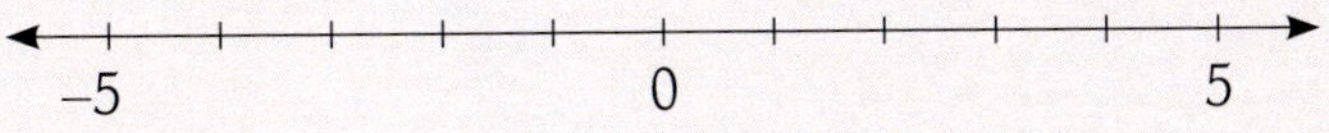

1. Plot Jovin and his opponents on the number line. Use the letters to label the points.
   - **a.** Jovin is at 0.
   - **b.** Kelly is 3 meters ahead of Jovin.
   - **c.** Nick is 1 meter behind Kelly.
   - **d.** Saul is 2 meters behind Jovin.
   - **e.** Chris is 3 meters behind Saul.
2. Which racers are in first and last place at this point in the race?
3. How can you tell how much distance is between the first and last place racers?
4. Name any racers who are the same distance from Jovin and how far from him they are.

Motocross racers crash into each other.

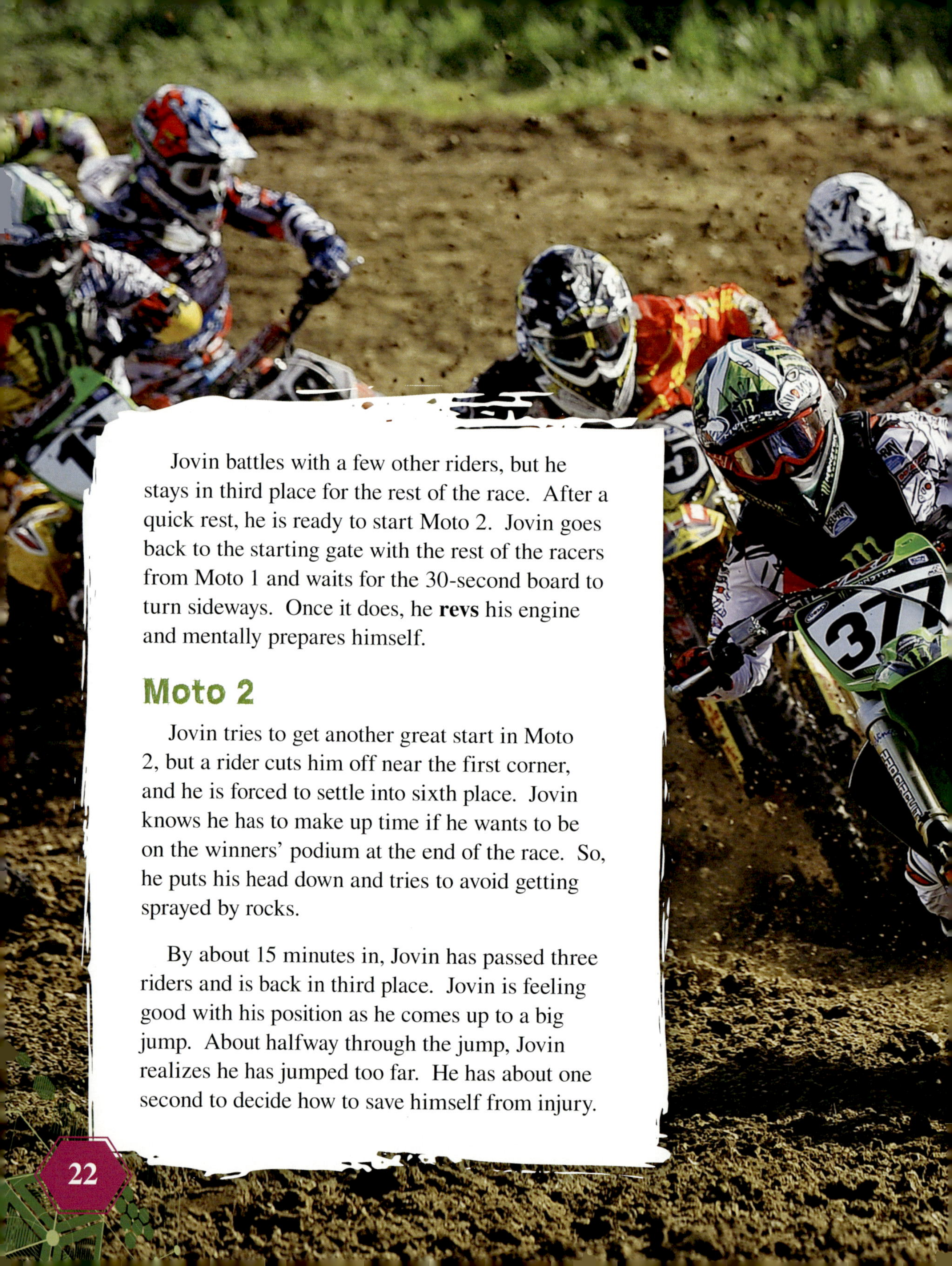

Jovin battles with a few other riders, but he stays in third place for the rest of the race. After a quick rest, he is ready to start Moto 2. Jovin goes back to the starting gate with the rest of the racers from Moto 1 and waits for the 30-second board to turn sideways. Once it does, he **revs** his engine and mentally prepares himself.

Moto 2

Jovin tries to get another great start in Moto 2, but a rider cuts him off near the first corner, and he is forced to settle into sixth place. Jovin knows he has to make up time if he wants to be on the winners' podium at the end of the race. So, he puts his head down and tries to avoid getting sprayed by rocks.

By about 15 minutes in, Jovin has passed three riders and is back in third place. Jovin is feeling good with his position as he comes up to a big jump. About halfway through the jump, Jovin realizes he has jumped too far. He has about one second to decide how to save himself from injury.

The first corner in any motocross race is one of the most dangerous spots on the track.

Jovin has two choices—stay on his bike or bail out. If Jovin stays on his bike, he will crash on flat ground, which could injure his feet, knees, hips, and back. Or, Jovin can bail out by purposely jumping off his dirt bike and trying to cushion his fall as best he can. In midair, Jovin makes a decision and bails off his dirt bike.

As other riders race past him, Jovin has one thing on his mind: he needs to land on his feet and let his momentum carry him through the fall. As his feet touch the dirt, Jovin tucks his head and somersaults forward. Fortunately, Jovin's training has helped him make the right choice, and he quickly jumps back up on his dirt bike.

Jovin finds himself in seventh place after the crash. He knows he has fewer than 15 minutes to catch and pass some of his fellow racers, so he powers forward and tries to ride fast while staying safe. Jovin passes one rider and then another and ends the race in fifth place. Jovin is happy with the result when he thinks back over the tough day he's had.

A motocross racer crashes in a corner.

MOTO 2

The Winners' Podium

Jovin eagerly waits for the final winners to be announced. He knows he will not be on the podium, but he is still curious to see how everyone else did. Finally, the riders' positions in the two races are combined and the results are announced. Jovin's third-place finish in Moto 1 and his fifth-place finish in Moto 2 give him an overall fourth-place finish.

Jovin celebrates a fun, safe, and successful race day. He knows what parts he did well on, and he knows what he needs to work on for the next race. He congratulates other riders and takes his plaque home to hang on his wall. Jovin has a lot of trophies and plaques from races he has won. Sometimes, he gives them away to other riders when he thinks they deserve them. Other times, he keeps them to remind himself to work hard for another win. The day after a race, Jovin relaxes with his friends and family. But on Tuesday, Jovin is back practicing for the next race, and his training starts all over again.

Jovin spends the day with his friends and family.

LET'S EXPLORE MATH

Imagine that these are average speeds for five amateur motocross racers in kilometers per hour.

1. Write all the average speeds in the same form, either fractions or decimals. Explain your choice.
2. Order the racers from fastest to slowest average speeds.

Racer	Average Speed (km/h)
Patrick	62.24
Sean	$62\frac{1}{5}$
Carmen	$\frac{125}{2}$
David	62.02
Alex	62.204

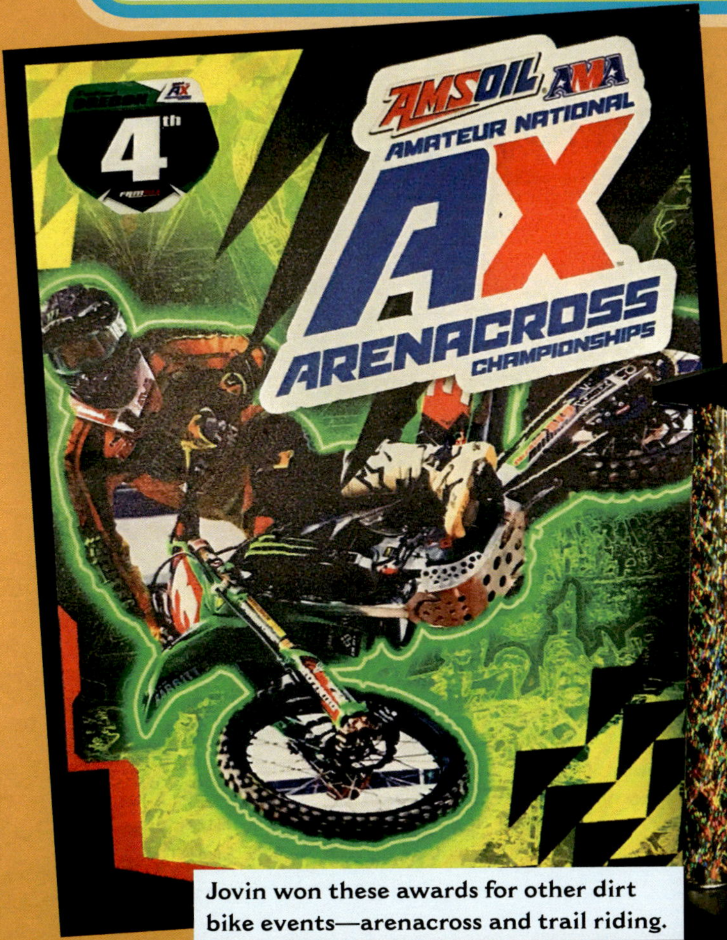

Jovin won these awards for other dirt bike events—arenacross and trail riding.

Problem Solving

Amateur motocross racers are excited when local businesses want to sponsor them. Sponsors might give racers gear. They might pay racers to wear their logos, use their gear, or make appearances in advertisements.

Imagine that you are a successful racer. After winning a race, local businesses want to start sponsoring you. You open a bank account so you can use the money to buy new gear. Your sponsors expect a report at the end of the week, showing how the money was spent. Draw a number line like the one on page 29. Use it with the list of earnings and expenses to track the balance in your account. Follow the guidelines to write the report for your sponsors.

Report Guidelines

The report must include:

- ❏ how much total money you earned and spent during the week;
- ❏ explanation of why financial activities are represented with negative or positive numbers;
- ❏ explanation of any times your account was overdrawn (had less than $0);
- ❏ when you had the most and least money;
- ❏ how much money you have at the end of the week; and
- ❏ whether you had more money after the amusement park commercial or at the end of the week.

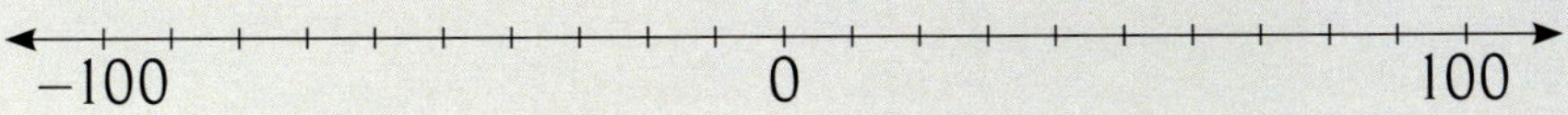

Earnings and Expenses

appeared in amusement park commercial: earned $100

purchased gloves online: spent $10

purchased pants at a new bike shop: spent $70

agreed to wear gas station logo during next race: earned $30

appeared at bike shop grand opening while wearing new pants: earned $15

purchased helmet: spent $90

photographed for motocross park poster: earned $40

Glossary

amateur—someone who does something for fun and not as a job

anticipation—a feeling of excitement because something is about to happen

class—a group of people who are at the same level of experience

coordination—the ability to move different body parts together well or easily

current—a continuous flow of air or water in the same direction

dehydrated—lost too much water in the body

dirt bike—a type of motorcycle that is designed to be used on rough surfaces

endurance—the ability to continue doing something difficult for a long time

facet—part of something

imperative—important

jolts—causes someone to move in a quick and sudden way

lithe—moving in a graceful and easy way

pristine—fresh, like new

regimen—a plan of rules about food and exercise to keep someone healthy

revs—causes an engine to run more quickly

ruts—long, narrow marks made by a lot of wheels passing over the same area

seize—to stop working

technicality—details that need to be understood to be successful

terrain—a certain kind of land

throttle—a device that controls the amount of fuel sent to an engine

traction—the force that causes moving things to grip the surface against which they are moving

tread—the pattern of raised lines on the outside of a tire

Index

Answer Key

Let's Explore Math

page 5

1. 3.25; $3\frac{1}{4}$, $\frac{13}{4}$, $3\frac{25}{100}$, or $\frac{325}{100}$.

2. 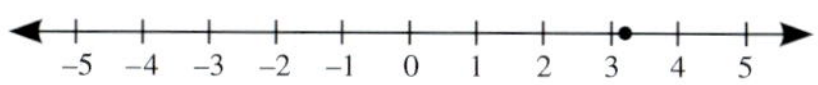

   Strategies may include estimating $3\frac{1}{2}$ and plotting $3\frac{1}{4}$ halfway between it and 3.

page 7

1. 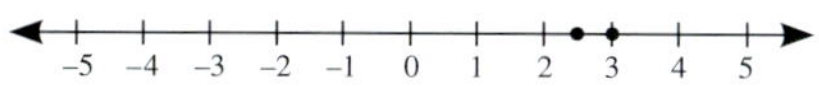

2. 3 minutes per lap

3. 3 is an integer because it is a number that can be written without a fractional part.

page 9

Scott uses the greatest amount and Rosa uses the least amount; Explanations may include that Scott's amount has 4 tenths, Rosa's has 0 tenths, and Kristina's has 3 tenths.

page 15

1. 0; Jovin's water gains and losses are tracked from this point.

2. Jovin lost 1 cup of water because the total at the end of the day is negative.

page 21

1. 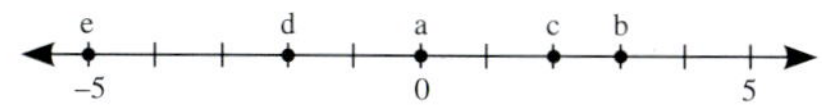

2. first place: Kelly; last place: Chris

3. Chris is 5 m behind Jovin and Kelly is 3 m ahead of Jovin for a total distance of 8 m.

4. Saul and Nick are both 2 m away.

page 27

1. $62\frac{24}{100}$, 62.2, 62.5; $62\frac{2}{100}$, $62\frac{204}{1,000}$; Writing the speeds as decimals makes them easier to compare.

2. Carmen, Patrick, Alex, Sean, David

Problem Solving

Reports should include: \$185 earned and \$170 spent; positive numbers represent money earned and negative numbers represent money spent; the account was overdrawn after purchasing the helmet, but more money was put in to cover the expense; the account had the most money (\$100) after appearing in the commercial and the least money (–\$25) after purchasing the helmet; the account had \$15 at the end of the week; and there was more money in the account at the beginning of the week.